The Vision of Wisdom

Holy Inspired by God
Volume I

Gerald Filyaw

The Vision of Wisdom: Holy Inspired by God Volume I
Gerald Filyaw

Scripture quotations marked KJV are from the KING JAMES VERSION of the Bible.

Scripture quotations marked (NLT) are taken from the Holy Bible, New Living Translation, copyright © 1996, 2004, 2007 by Tyndale House Foundation. Used by permission of Tyndale House Publishers, Inc., Carol Stream, Illinois 60188. All rights reserved.

Published by ◤◥DiViNE PURPOSE PUBLISHING CO. LLC

Website: www.divinepurposepublishing.com
Email: info@divinepurposepublishing.com

Miracle of the Loaves and Fish ®

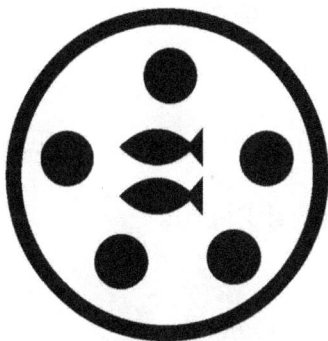

This logo is a representation of the
Miracle of the Five Loaves and Two Fish
based on the scripture Matthew 14:13-21

Miracle of the Loaves & Fish logo is a registered trademark

For apparel, jewelry, household goods and more with this logo, go to: http://cafepress.com/miracleofloavesnfish

Miracle of the Loaves and Fish ® Shop
Expect a miracle - -everyday!
Matthew 14:13-21

Table of Contents

Dedication

This book is personally dedicated to each person who picks it up to read. To the whole world around the globe, to people of every nation, please let God change your life, just as He has changed my life.

God tailored this book for you. God had you in mind when He divinely inspired this wonderful and powerful book of blessings.

I pray that today, you will start your new life in Christ Jesus. Trust God. You have never felt love like this before today. Let God wake you up from a dead life of sin.

Only God can help you, you have tried all your life and could not do it. It's your day, a new day to find God's way for life.

Foreword

In times past, Holy men of God, were inspired by God to write the Holy scriptures of the Bible. **2 Timothy 3:16-17 (KJV)** All scripture is given by inspiration of God, and is profitable for doctrine, for reproof, for correction, for instruction in righteousness: That the man of God may be perfect, thoroughly furnished unto all good works.

God has not changed. He is the same God yesterday, today and forever. Just as He spoke back in the Old and New Covenant (Testament), He is still speaking today.

As I read The Vision of Wisdom Volume I could not put this book down. The words ministered to my spirit, spoke to my heart and there was an impartation of a greater understanding of who God is and what He expects from His children.

As you read you will know that this wisdom is not wisdom from nor of man, but these writings of wisdom can only come from God. You will become enlightened and your spirit will become full as you read these words from the heart and mind of God.

LaShawn Dobbs

Introduction

The Vision of Wisdom is Holy Inspired by God. God speaks according to His Word that has already been written (The Holy Bible). He will not speak anything contrary to His already written Word. Every word that is written in The Vision of Wisdom is in sync with God's already written Word.

Before reading, pray and ask God to give you knowledge and understanding of what you're about to read. Without seeking God first, these words of wisdom will not make sense to the carnal mind.

The Word of God speaks of this in **1 Corinthians 2:14 (NLT)** But people who aren't spiritual can't receive these truths from God's Spirit. It all sounds foolish to them and they can't understand it, for only those who are spiritual can understand what the Spirit means.

God gave me 'The Vision of Wisdom' over the last eleven years, (2003-2014) after I sought Him asked Him for wisdom. This book is Volume I of III.

There is much that I do understand and then there are some that I, myself, still have not received the wisdom to understand exactly what God is saying, but as I continue to read and seek Him, He grants unto me more understanding of what He is saying.

Therefore, I encourage you to seek God. Ask God for knowledge, wisdom and understanding. In the book of James; **James 1:5 (NLT)** it is written "If you need wisdom, ask our generous God, and he will give it to you. He will not rebuke you for asking."

After you pray and ask God for knowledge, wisdom and understanding, believe that He has heard you and by faith receive because that's what you asked Him for.

As you read The Vision of Wisdom, allow the words of wisdom to minister to your heart and mind. Don't try to figure it out carnally, if there's something you read that you don't understand, ask God for understanding.

There were several times God had given me a phrase and the next sentence or sometimes a couple days later, He would give me what seemed like the same phrase all over again, but once I went back and read the two phrases I realized, though they were alike they were not totally the same. At first I could not understand why God was repeating Himself, just in a different manner.

He then let me know—we learn by repetition, the more we hear or read something it will take root in us. Hence, His reason for doing this is because He is depositing His wisdom in us, not wisdom from man, but He is depositing—His wisdom in us as we take in His words.

I know that "The Vision of Wisdom" will bless you just as it has blessed me, because these words are Holy Inspired by God, this wisdom is not of my own, but from Him.

As you read, you too will know that the mind of man could not fathom what God is saying, therefore it had to come from Him.

Thank God for a spiritual mind to understand the things of the spirit.

God Bless!

If you want to know who God is, learn who Jesus is too.

Without Christ your life is upside down and a mess, but with Christ, it's right side up and blessed.

Disobedience took my life, but obedience gave it back.

Obedience will open doors that disobedience has closed shut.

Christians never stop repenting, but they can stop repenting for the same sins over again.

To repeat what the bible says, is not judging, it's repeating what God says.

Obedience shows visible proof of who we are in Christ.

I don't need a religion that teaches me to sin, I had enough of that.

When you think of right, think of daytime. When you think of wrong think of nighttime.

Negative talk brings a negative walk.

Don't use your fists, use your faith.

When you are full of God you are full of love because God is love.

If God is in you looking out from your eyes, you would not want to look at sin.

If you buy anything you know is stolen then you're just a bad as the thief, you give him a reason to steal.

Stop asking how and let God happen.

God is the only one who can change something bad into something good.

When God speaks, shut up!

If you want a life, then don't hang around a person who doesn't have one.

The beginning of honor, is honoring God's Word first.

No matter how much the devil disagrees, you agree with God.

The Holy Highway is not a two way street, it's only one way, Holy.

People who treat you wrong, are wrong for you.

How can God renew your mind, if you do not read His Word into your mind?

If God ordered it, you should eat it.

If you love God, then you love His Word, His Word is His character.

When you're wrong, all the talking in the world will not make you right.

When a man is never wrong, something is wrong.

When a man thinks he's never wrong, he's thinking wrong.

Pride hates correction.

If you live in the past, your future is dead.

Positive start helps create a positive finish.

The devil wants you to focus on the outside to forget the battles on the inside.

The devil wants you to think backwards to walk backwards.

God wants to correct what the world has recked. Don't use your words and then think, think before you use your words.

Don't disgrace God's grace. Don't sell your soul for the price of sin.

Saints that are around sinners all the time, are attracted to their ways.

People who laugh at you, one day you will cry for them.

Once you lock into faith, don't unlock it.

God put in you what He needs to get from you.

Sinful friends will not help you stay saved, they will only help you to backslide.

Your life will show the evidence of who you serve.

Sin has to be evil, and it has to be bad, or it would not be sin. God will give you a set free guarantee, He guarantees He'll set you free.

The devil will show you what's fake, but God will show you what's real.

When you shake the devil's hand, he won't let go, you need God to break his grip.

If you don't want to steal, kill and destroy with the devil, then call on the name of the Lord.

There are two types of seeds, good seeds and bad seeds. Don't plant bad seeds. A good seed will bless you, but a bad seed will curse you.

I must confess, when you're blessed, you get blessed. You have to do God's will His way or it will not be His will. When you have God, God has you.

I'm trying to help someone from going to hell. Just because you're walking that way doesn't mean God cannot turn you around.

Now faith means that we are now people. There is nothing late in now faith.

The devil will help you the wrong way. God will help you the right way. The devil wants to help you the wrong way, but God will help you the right way.

The bridge you burn, is your own. The bridge you burn, you own. A fools bridge will always burn, he has nothing to cross back on.

Fear the Lord, not the devil. The devil will make your mouth your enemy, but God will make your mouth your friend.

Now faith doesn't mean later faith, it means now, right now in the present.

Your choices determine your courses. Christians are not supposed to let the devil direct their paths.

A fireman's job is to get people out of the fire, then to put the fire out. God desires to get you out and put out the fires in your life.

The reason why we have to guard our hearts is because freewill allows our hearts to change back to sinning.

My bible says in **Proverbs 3:5-6** *Emphasis in parenthesis added* "Trust in the Lord with all thine heart (not satan); and lean not unto thine own understanding. ⁶ In all thy ways acknowledge Him, and He shall (means God will) direct thy paths.

All the paths that God direct, lead to God. When you lose your way, you fall away; out of the way.

When we fail God, it's not because God failed us.

Sin will never be sinless, it will always be sinful.

God has made you sinless, so you should sin less.

God made you sinless, not to sin more, but to sin less.

You should know, that no is a blessing, when it comes from God.

There's a difference between religious and just being plainly in love with God.

Every miracle is great and there is none small.

Freedom is not where you're at, freedom is in Christ. Freedom is everywhere Jesus is and that's everywhere.

When God blesses you, everyone who is obedient will bless you. When God blesses you, even sinners will bless you.

To have a new life, you have to become a new life. To have a new life, you have to become a new creation in Christ Jesus the Lord.

Do you want a new life? I'm trying to tell you the direction of correction.

You have to have faith that God's Words automatically has strength and power.

Jesus speaks words of strength and power, you have to speak words of strength and power.

When you seek evil you find evil, but when you seek righteousness you find God's Son, Jesus Christ the Lord.

"**<u>NOW</u>**" faith brings **NOW** action, that's why your faith has to be right now faith.

Faith is driving the planet earth—in the atmosphere, as it keeps the sun perfect.

As you move into the future your faith has to also move into the future with you. You cannot leave it behind, it has to be with you. Moment by moment, in every moment of your life.

Your flesh has to become one with your spirit and with the Spirit, which is God's Spirit in you.

Your faith is your freewill; believing God's will freely.

God is not only a rocket scientist, He is also a planet scientist. He created everything. There would not be a planet to go to if God did not plan it.

Don't let the devil plant in your garden, he will tell you it's roses, but you'll end up with weeds.

The devil is like a cockroach, he loves darkness and runs from the light.

The devil is like a weed; he keeps coming back, no matter how many times you weed whack him down with the Word of God.

The Lord of the Word is the Word of the Lord.

If the body is not working together it is not The Body.

If your life is upside down let God turn it around.

When you put God in it you put the devil out of it.

The devil cannot last when you fast.

God is all about love and He wants you to be all about love.

There will be no pride in hell.

When you love the Lord, you love the Word, He is the Word.

If you're doing the desires of the devil, you want to do them because you have freewill.

Your greatest need, is needing God.

Almost every time you're getting ready to get blessed, here comes the devil's mess.

The devil can try his best, but we have the Lord's best.

If I fail, the Word won't fail. If I mess up the Word won't mess up.

You can form the weapon of love, right now, against the enemy.

Man's love is not agape and it will never be agape, in this flesh.

Agape love is perfect, it will never mess up, but we mess up.

God sees the agape love of Jesus on the inside of us.

When you make God your greatest need, He takes care of all of your needs.

Your problems are crumbs in God's hands.

You're nothing without God, because when you were without God you were nothing.

You should be mad enough to love everyone by now. The devil should have you loving like mad.

We know that God sees through, but is He getting through to you.

When you hate, you serve out hate and the devil serves in hate. While you hate others, the devil hates you, it is a hate to hate relationship.

Walking in the Word, is walking in the works.

God sees through you, He sees your spirit, which is you.

What you cannot handle, God will handle.

The devil's job is to hate you and get you to hate yourself.

Ask God to save you, to behave, like you're saved.

Disobedience starts in the mind and ends in the flesh.

You have to battle in your mind, to protect your life. You have to battle in your mind, to protect your flesh.

If you don't stop negative thoughts, you start negative faults. Your thoughts become your faults.

Christ paid the price, for you to have His mind.

Don't buy the lie. You have to know the signs to protect your mind.

God never had an impure thought, you have to stop your stinking thinking.

The devil hates you and wants you to hate yourself. God loves you and wants you to love yourself.

God wants you to live, the devil wants you to die.

Your readiness to desire God, should be the same to completion.

Grace has nothing to do with dis-grace.

The mind of Christ is the mind of God. A pure mind is a God controlled mind. Christ obeyed God's mind.

When you follow the wrong thoughts, they become your faults. Let the thoughts of God guard your heart.

God's Word is life and it will never die.

When you are born again, God changes your nature into His supernatural.

You are born again into a miracle and that miracle is Jesus.

When you are ordained, you are ordered.

When your natural and God's supernatural come together, you are no longer natural.

God loves you so much, that the potter is willing to live inside the clay—with you, that's love brother.

Just because you live inside dirt (this body), doesn't mean you have to live like dirt.

I don't care how much you wash the outside, only God can wash the inside.

When God cleans the inside, the outside starts to look cleaner.

I praise God through what I'm going through and for what I am going through.

Is your mind set to be reset?

The miracle of the loaves and fish was God and it's still God.

There's a liar that's alive and his name is the devil. But there's a real God that's alive, the God of righteousness, the God of heaven and earth.

God is the miracle who creates the miracles.

The world would rather believe a liar, they don't want to believe an honest plan. What's wrong with this planet?

When God thanks you with a blessing, I believe a blessing is God's way of saying "well done."

When the Father said "well done" to His son, that was higher than saying "thank you."

Do you know how God says "thank you?" By saying "well done." God says "thank you" when He says "well done."

The devil wants you strung out, then he wants your time to run out.

The miracle of the loaves and fish, is the miracle of God.

When God is in your heart, love is in your heart; because God is love.

If hate is in your heart, then God is not in your heart. God's not hate, He's love.

Peoples opinions don't count if it's not faith.

God is the miracle in front of every miracle.

The righteous answer with the Fruit of the Spirit.

Peoples opinions should not matter to you if they're not faith.

Faith doesn't wait, people wait. Faith is always ready, waiting for you to become ready.

Your mind is armed and dangerous, when it puts the Word into action.

The righteous answer with the Fruit of the Spirit.

When you do not work, your faith will not work.

You have to obey God, past your negative thoughts which is past your understanding.

You can understand more than most people understand. You can understand and still not know anything.

You have to look past things that won't last.

Where there's no love, there's no light. Where there's no light, there's no life.

Are you really iron or metal plated?

The pleasures of this world pass away the same day.

Backbiting is the devil's lunch.

God will not bless your mess, He will bless your best.

Wisdom answers wisely. You can tell if a man has wisdom by the way he answers.

Anger knows no wisdom and never speaks wisely.

When you pass your understanding, then you know what God wants you to understand.

Anger never agrees with wisdom, but it loves the fool.

Without God you cannot pass your understanding, but with God you can pass your understanding.

Only the devil will tell you not to say everything that God has told you to speak.

Love your backbiters too, for they warn you when the enemy is attacking you.

Faith looks past the negative and finds the positive.

Faith seeks the positive, or it would not be faith.

Faith attacks everything negative.

If you didn't have some enemies, you would not be a Christian.

When your heart desires more right than wrong, you're getting stronger.

Trust starts small and grows large, but so does deceit.

I am not your enemy and I'm not "the enemy," but your enemy told you it's me.

I'm not your enemy, but the enemy will tell you that I'm your enemy. If you believe the enemy, you're with the enemy.

Not everyone will like what you say, but that's okay, say it God's way.

Some Christians will say "I'm not God," when they should say "I have God."

Sometimes when people don't understand you, they can't stand you, but I'm still standing.

The devil hates to hear a Christian say "I love you."

You have to live passed your flesh into the spiritual.

You have to pass your flesh to get to the spiritual.

God waits on us more than we wait on Him.

God's long suffering is perfect, our long suffering is not.

Some people know more than you think, because they think more than you know.

If a person is mad about what God did for you, the devil's mad.

The fruit of the Spirit is in the heart of the righteous.

Some Christians will only have a few things, because they're not faithful over the few things.

Things that don't last, only last in your mind, which also doesn't last.

Christians fight better than sinners.

In the fruit of the Spirit, is the Spirit of the fruit.

A person that does what God says, doesn't care about negative things man say.

Death is near, but life is here, in Christ.

God can give you everything good, but the devil cannot give you anything good.

Be careful to guard your thoughts, because your thoughts could be weapons against you.

We think we are logical, but the only time we are logical is with God's logics.

The time you sow, it starts to grow.

Negative people will create negativity in the most positive things.

The beginning of negativity is a negative mind.

God is the creator of innovation. Innovation means nothing without motivation.

Sometimes we think the things God has done were illogical, until the logic results appear.

Love expresses itself in words and deeds.

The devil is illogical, but God is logical.

Acting on ungodly thoughts, changes Godly directions.

Obedience is loving God and acting on it.

When a person can never be wrong, something isn't right.

When a leader can never be wrong, something isn't right.

There is nothing right about doing what is wrong, all wrong doing is evil.

Some people, when they're wrong, think that they can talk themselves right.

When you love the Lord, you love to do His words.

Doing wrong is evil because wrong is not good.

There is nothing good in doing wrong, you will only find more wrong in wrong.

If you're not doing righteousness then you're doing unrighteousness—there only exists good and evil.

If God ordered it, it's an order.

Doing unrighteousness is evil, doing unrighteousness is not righteous.

The devil wants your past to last, so he could harass.

How can you know right if you don't know wrong; or righteousness if you don't know unrighteousness?

You can see a man's heart by what you hear.

The devil tries to fool you into believing that your past is your future.

Keep your faith, only the unfaithful goes in the opposite direction.

A form of godliness, does not form godliness.

If you tell a person he is good when doing bad, you don't bless him, you curse him.

If you can discern good, you can discern evil.

Freewill was created to obey faith.

Every step may look small, but with faith, it's tall.

A person who shuns evil, is not evil.

The opposite of faith is death.

You know the devil lies, so don't believe your past is your future.

If you want to live, you better live to suffer.

When you tell a person he is good when he is bad, you curse him.

To practice sinning does not make you better in righteousness.

Repentance does not mean "stay the same," it means change.

There's a reason for your vision, because every vision has a reason.

You have to have wisdom to see your vision from God.

Some people don't see what they have, they only see what they don't have.

When God says "now," it means right now.

A person who practices sinning is losing.

You don't know what your future holds, but one thing for sure, God holds your future.

Let your walk worship God.

You were created for good, not evil.

Faith is believing before you see.

Correction keeps you in the right direction.

Lord, thank You for waking me up out of sin and waking me up into righteousness.

Whatever you've been through, is through in Christ.

God controls the earth; how can your problems be too big for God?

Problems that are seen are like vapor and steam.

You will only find right in righteousness.

Faith sees passed places and conditions.

The vision of division, is the vision of satan.

If you are walking in division, you have walked out of your vision.

A person who defends sinning—is sinning.

The devil wants you to forget what he put you through, so he can do it again.

When you step in God's hands, you're steps are in God's hands.

Don't defend sinning, defend from sinning.

When Christians say "I cannot be perfect," you can't be because you don't believe you can.

The words you choose can make you win or lose.

When we obey, we don't pay, but when we disobey we pay. You don't have to pay, unless you disobey.

At the cross there's no disobedience.

You have to want to be obedient to be obedient.

You have to want to be obedient for your faith to help you be obedient.

Nothing from nothing, leaves nothing and if you try it, it will leave you nothing.

God placed your spiritual gifts in you for you to use your spiritual gifts. God put your physical gifts in you for you to use your physical gifts.

I don't care how much food you look at, you will never become full until you eat some.

The weak will say "I can't be perfect," but faith never says "I can't be perfect," because faith agrees with God.

When you say "I can't be perfect" the problem is you say you can't.

31

If you hate evil, you won't be evil.

It's alright to hate sin, but it's not alright to hate people.

What sense does this make; people who hate sin hanging around people who love sin?

Some people read the Word, but they don't eat the Word.

You don't get full of the Word by reading, you get full of the Word by doing.

When you say that you can't be perfect; you're calling God a liar.

Whatever is going on in your life God is allowing it; for His reason and the reasons in your lifetime.

Whatever is in your life is for your life. Whatever is in your life is for your life or it wouldn't be in your life.

When you speak the words "I can't," you live the words "I can't."

Love looks beyond hate and still loves all.

God knows what we need before we know we need anything.

God never forgets to remember.

If you look in God's mirror, you can see your image.

God obeys your freewill.

Jesus told the world, "God is in Me and He is the one that is Me."

It's easy for anybody to be like everybody else, but it's hard for anybody not to be like everybody else.

God will let you go through everything, so you'll love Him more than everything.

Sin is nobody's friend, not even the devils.

Your reflection should reflect perfection.

Love, loves to be friendly.

You can understand more when you listen, don't let your mouth interrupt your ears.

If perfection were an apple and you were hungry; would you not climb the tree to eat? Well, keep climbing to eat perfection.

God knows what we need before we need what He knows.

The devil will make you look like death, but God will make you look like life.

Problems are the best teachers.

Faith takes what is negative and turns it into positive.

Faith is not a friend of negativity.

Faith looks past the natural into the supernatural.

You cannot walk in light and darkness too, where there's light there is no darkness.

Just because you say "I'm saved," doesn't make you saved.

Disobedience is rejecting obedience.

Negatives are weak, but positives are stronger.

Faith shows the devil where to go.

When faith shows, the devil has to go, because faith is in the light.

A form of godliness does not form godliness.

You have to look past things that won't last into things that will last.

What we think is impossible, faith knows it's possible.

Your mouth can be an enemy against your ears.

When you surround yourself with positive people, something positive has already happened.

If you want to have something, stay away from people who don't want to have anything.

If you want to stay clean, stay away from people who want to stay dirty.

When God dials your number, pick up the phone.

In this life, for whatever you do, you either get paid or pay.

God really enjoys your freewill love for Him.

Anything that's not Godly is not golden.

Anything that is negative, is not positive.

Negativity will fall, but positivity will stand.

It is safe to covet your covenant.

In life, the direction you take is the direction you make.

With a positive start, you have a positive finish.

Why are you climbing that mountain when you can move it?

People going nowhere, have nowhere to take you.

Don't practice climbing mountains, practice moving them.

We are transformed to be in God's form now, we make it a process.

You cannot lift spiritual burdens with physical strength.

God knows everything, but He's not going to force you to do anything.

A person who obeys evil, obeys death.

If your mirror is clean, then you can clean other mirrors.

When God is in front of you, He will put good people behind you.

To succeed, find a need.

A work of art, comes from the art of work.

You don't know a person until you live with them, then you may wish you never knew them at all.

Prayer without obedience is just air.

In life it doesn't matter what people think, it's up to you to swim or sink.

How can you stand, if you do not understand.

God sees Jesus inside your heart.

Who can help you without God helping you?

Jesus is the light that gives you life.

If you believe that you're saved, help your actions to believe.

When you're around, you're sound.

The Word is a sword and a sword is a weapon.

The closer you get to God, the more you'll see God's hand.

Faith is an obedient word.

The closer you get to God, the brighter you get from God.

Witness the world, drugs are a door that's hard to close.

The beginning of success is forgetting failures.

If you're not positive, it's not possible.

Problems that are seen are like vapors and steam—they don't last.

Faith is perfect and everything it touches becomes perfect.

Success and failure are enemies, when one comes the other leaves.

You were born infected, re-born corrected.

When God makes you happy, no man can hurt you.

Drugs are the practice of weakness.

The Word of God how good it sounds, the Word of God, how is your ground?

You don't get full of the Word by reading your bible, you get full of the Word by doing your bible.

Obedience is loving God in action.

Do you speak, who you seek?

If you plant a seed, you will get what you need.

There is wisdom that is wise and there is wisdom that are lies.

The devil will use anybody to attack anybody that does not know they are being used.

NEWSFLASH: When you walk outside of your bible, you have walked outside of God.

Your life should be the evidence of what you speak.

We resist the devil by disagreeing with him by God's Word.

A positive start, starts the positive finish.

God watches who takes advantage of His kindness inside His people.

Real success is winning Christ.

When you deal with actuality, only then do you deal with reality.

When you deal with actuality, you deal with reality.

Problems are like questions, they have answers too.

Don't climb what you can move.

When you hear about other peoples problems, your problems become weak.

If you are reborn back out of this world, you shouldn't act like this world.

Faith does not make excuses.

Christians should not make excuses to live a sinful life. Christians should make excuses to live a righteous life.

Making excuses can be sinful.

Faith is the solution to preventing excuses.

It is better to cry than to lie.

Disobedience is unfaithful, how can you walk in faith?

When you come into this world you need to be reborn back out of this world.

When an argument starts subtle and then blows up, that's the devil in you.

The devil does not care who's right or wrong, he just wants their anger.

When you argue who's right or wrong, you're both wrong.

A fools mouth taste no wisdom, while a wise man eats contently.

The devil knows that as long as Christians fight each other they cannot fight against him.

The devil hates friendship, only evil is his friend.

Don't talk people to death, talk people to life.

What looks like a problem to you, is a problem to you; because it looks like a problem to you.

You have to faith, the end result good.

Start looking at what looks like a problem, not like a problem by faith.

Faith sees the problem, but sees past the problem to God who is the solution.

Your flesh cannot see what your spiritual eye can see, so your flesh needs to obey your spirit.

Faith does not look for a solution, faith is the solution.

Whatever you've done wrong in life, "plant good," to make things good.

Negativity is disobedience and positivity is obedience.

The beginning of perfection is the end of disobedience.

Some people talk God, but you can't see our God in them.

In your life don't look at the "cant's," look at the can's, the things you can do.

To see God in a person you must see His characteristics.

The voice of a hypocrite scatters.

Faith is like an eraser that eradicates problems.

If you have faith, no matter what it looks like it looks like faith.

Faith sees faith. Situations and conditions does not change faith.

When you know faith is the answer you don't need to ask questions.

When you know faith is the answer you don't seek the answer.

Faith knocks on God's door.

Negativity is the opposite of positivity and negativity is sin.

Anything that's not holy is unholy.

If you don't have love, you don't have God because God is love.

How can you talk love when you don't walk love?

Some people will talk the Word, but they're as wicked as the devil.

There is nothing bad in a good seed.

When a person turns back to sin, God doesn't listen; Why should I?

Obedience is better than disobedience.

Some talk God, but you see another god in their walk.

Obedience is not for salvation, but it's evidence of salvation.

If you don't have any evidence of salvation then you have no salvation.

Everything in a Christian's life, God allows to help them.

The devil wants you to look at other people's faults and forget your faults.

You know, your prayers are not an abomination when you obey God.

You know that your prayers are not an abomination because you obey God.

Some people call willfully sinning obeying God, they believe that they're saved.

A resurrected lifestyle is resurrected away from disobedience.

If you don't show God, you don't know God.

How can you preach the Word, when you cannot teach the Word?

When God is on your side, He's on your inside.

If you focus on the things you can't do, more than the things you can do, you won't do the things you can do.

It may not look like a blessing, but understand, in Christ, adversity is a blessing that will help you.

Only a liar would say "I don't need God."

God knows how much you love Him, but love always wants to show love.

Are you weak enough to die and strong enough to cry?

Sinners will talk like love, but they can't walk in love.

Your past, doesn't have to be your future.

People who feel small, generally, will talk bigger than they feel.

The higher you think, the higher you rank. The lower you think, the lower you sink.

Let God make you into who He created you to become.

Let God make you into who He created.

If you're not meek, you're weak.

God can keep you if you want to be kept.

Let God make you into who you're supposed to be.

Every time you disobey, you're doing things the other way. Every time you disobey, you're doing things the old way.

How can you do things God's way, if you're still doing things your way?

You were born needing people, that's why you have parents.

First the devil trick you to fight, then he convinces you to backbite.

Faith speaks "it's gonna rain," even if you've never seen rain before in your life.

Your will walks together with your faith.

Faith says "it's gonna rain," and as long as you wait, it's still faith.

A part of resisting the devil is resisting the flesh, not just your flesh, but all flesh.

Everything you've been through, wasn't just for you, it was for God too.

Strongholds are attacks to destroy your future.

Christians talk about generational curses, but not about the generational blessings.

God is excited, you never know what He's gonna do in your life next!

I don't care how much faith you have, it means nothing without your will.

You were born passing through this world, because time passes through.

Sin is too selfish to care about anything.

If you want to be on fire for God, be obedient.

Your will has to walk together with your faith.

The world use fear to control people, Christians use faith to restore people.

You cannot use flesh for faith.

The world use hate to control everything. Christians use love to control everything.

It's always exciting when it's relationship. It's always boring when it's religion, because religion is sinful.

A relationship is never boring when you do things together.

Faith and fear will never share.

Your seed is not just for your need.

Humility never says "remember this, remember that."

Forget what you don't have and remember who you do have.

You can have faith, but you need to have focused faith.

When you look at women sinfully, you don't look at God righteously.

No matter how much you learn, you have to learn to obey first.

God reminds us, because He knows that sin is attacking our memories.

Don't let nobody's past or present destroy your future with God.

God's way is God's will and we need to will God's way.

I cannot say what tomorrow brings, but I can say "God brings tomorrow."

You can operate in all of your spiritual gifts at the same time.

God will not abuse you, just use you.

Christians don't love people for their actions, they love them for God's actions.

Are you praising God to be seen or because you're not ashamed?

There are no good liars, they're all bad.

A liar is a deceiver.

Nobody is always wrong. Nobody is always right, but God…

Simplicity avoids complications.

Obedience is righteous.

The only way you can live smart, is with a Godly heart.

Behavior without restrictions causes destruction.

The only thing you can do without God is sin.

There is no satisfaction in words without action.

What you sow will show.

How can we be better if we don't stick together?

Don't hate negative people, hate their negativity.

Less homes, create homeless.

Anytime you deal with people you deal with problems, because people have problems.

When you believe what you believe, that's all you receive.

Just because you love Jesus doesn't mean people are gonna love you.

When you have "God's seed," you have more than you need.

Suffering for a Christian is good, because it's allowed by God.

First comes knowledge then comes wisdom.

Forgiveness forgets faults.

When you have God's Son you've already won.

Drugs are where your future ends and where your end begins.

Don't let the devil control you, you control the devil.

Wisdom makes knowledge complete.

Never ask a fool how to be wise.

When you see your best, it comes form being blessed.

The answer to your prayers start with a relationship with your maker.

Reality starts with genuineness.

The answer to your prayers start with a relationship with God.

The door of the prison, is the gate of the fool.

A great man knows that he is not great, but his God is great.

Learn from how God treats you, how to treat others.

If God did not forgive you, you would not have the power to forgive yourself.

The doors of the prison, laugh and wait for the foolish.

What you try to prove, sometimes proves to be foolish.

God has placed in motion the laws of sowing and reaping, for your involvement (faith).

If you do good, you get good. If you do bad, you get bad, whether saved or unsaved.

When you change your way of thinking, your thinking changes your ways.

When you change your path of thinking, your path of thinking will change your paths.

God knows everything and we know nothing without God.

Every crime starts with a negative mind.

Negative people are dangerous, because negativity is dangerous.

The path to right thinking is righteousness.

When you need an answer, go to God.

A person who does not forgive, shows how weak he is.

When you read, you reap from the Word.

Solutions exist for problems.

Solutions were created for problems.

When a problem comes up, solution beats it down.

Problems are sad, but solutions are happy.

God created a solution for every problem.

You cannot do God's will without God's power.

You have to put "I love you God," into action.

You don't have to respect my opinion, you have to respect God for giving us our own.

You don't have to disrespect someone's opinion, you can disagree respectfully.

A gift from the heart is a smart start. A gift from the heart is always smart.

If you live a lie in this life, you will live the same lie into eternal life.

When you direct your ways to God, He will direct your way.

When you direct your ways to God, He will direct blessings your way.

When you put self, on the shelf, you're not walking by yourself.

Faith is friendly, but fear is fierce.

Don't make a friendship a worship.

Faith is an invisible connection to heaven.

Faith fly's—lies fall.

Excuses make it easy to sin.

Love knows that people make mistakes.

What your mouth says—your body obeys.

Holy Inspired Poems

In this section, the next seven pages are poems. These poems are written just as God gave them to me. I pray that you have been blessed by this book.

Again, this is Volume I of III, keep a look out for Volumes II and III of *'The Vision of Wisdom: Holy Inspired by God'* coming soon.

Incarnation

From the heaven to the earth,
angels singing at His birth.
Name above every name,
Jesus Christ, God gave fame.
From rich to poor, left it all,
it was the time, for God to call.
Incarnation in His hand,
saved us all,
for the promised land.

Blessings

Blessings are rewards from right, sent down from the Lord of light, Glorious given in His hand, reach down to this earthly land. Happiness in His heart of gifts, words are true speak not of myths. Do your best to pass the test and make it to His place of rest.

Seek God's Help

Life is full of right and wrong, we all sing this same song, not one of us knows it all, we make mistakes from Adam's fall, so seek the Lord and get it right, The Holy Word the path of light, He'll change your life, relax in Him wash away your sins, He'll carry them.

Righteous Ark

Countenance, bright, sunshine, He is
God, He is mine, lift my hands, praise His
name, love You Lord, not ashamed.
Hallelujah, with a shout, fleeing demons,
leaving out. I AM SAVED from the dark,
light of Jesus, righteous Ark.

My God

My God, My God is so sweet,
problems I lay at His feet.
Loving heart wants to share,
who but God would be so fair.
Answers waiting always there,
divine wisdom lots of care.

He Paid the Price

Devil trick me, getting high,
to destroy my mind, hope I die.
Drugs and alcohol was my fall,
open my heart, heaven call.
Jesus Christ paid the price,
no more life of rolling dice.

The End of the Road

Now that I come towards the end of the road, life been up and down like the leap of a toad.

The Vision of Wisdom Artwork by Gerald Filyaw

New York Street Show

The Basement Artist

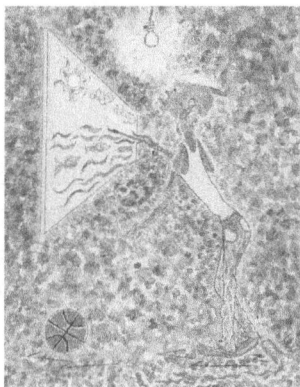

to view/purchase more artwork go to:
http://gerald-filyaw.pixels.com

Acknowledgements

I give all of the credit and glory to God because He is the power who inspired this book. Thank you Lord for creating this awesome book.

Special Thanks To:

My wonderful gifts from God, Shane, Priscilla, Kandyce, Sonny, Kelly, Duane, Jermaine and LaShawn, I love you all. My children, who have been through hell and high waters with me. Their love and forgiving hearts have blessed my life. Please forgive me for not being a better Dad years ago, but now I AM HEALED!!!

My mom and dad with all their love and understanding by faith and God, the only creator. God bless them, Rev. William G. Filyaw and wife Evangelist Geraldine Filyaw, who God used to help shape me, support me and raise me. I am so glad they're both in God's abode, Heaven.

My loving kind brother, William Filyaw Jr., who never stopped writing me every month, for nine years of prison. Your letters made me feel and know that you love me. I thank God for your true heart.

About the Author

Gerald Filyaw was born in New Haven, CT. to Pastor William G. Filyaw and Evangelist Geraldine Filyaw. Gerald spent most of his childhood in church.

When he was not in church he could be found on the basketball court. When Gerald was 11 years old, he began inventing and still enjoys inventing today.

Gerald started drinking alcohol at the age of 19, married at 20 and by the age of 21, he found himself addicted to using cocaine for over the next 26 years of his life.

His ungodly behavior ended in prison. It was at that time of solitude in his life that he received an awaking from God.

In 2003 he asked God for wisdom and God did just that, he gave Gerald Godly wisdom, it was then that The Vision of Wisdom began to come about.

Over the next eleven years, as God poured into Gerald (and He still does till this day) whatever paper he could find, and even inside the blank cover of his bible he would use it to write down the wisdom he receives.

Gerald is a high school drop out, but that did not paralyze God in the least from being able to use him for His glory. God is able to use anyone who will obey Him, to manifest His glory through and Gerald is grateful that God chose him.

Gerald has been given many gifts, one of which is an artist. His artwork has been displayed in art shows, public buildings,   public schools and newspaper articles. The word of his art continues to quickly spread, as he continues to submit his gifts unto God.

Gerald Filyaw is a born again believer, father, inventor and artist. He has eight wonderful children that he has been blessed with, whom he loves dearly.

Author Contact Information

Email all inquiries to:
gfilyaw@divinepurposepublishing.com
Subject: Attention Gerald Filyaw

Publisher Contact Information

DIVINE PURPOSE PUBLISHING Co., LLC
'WRITING WITH A PURPOSE'

DiVINE PURPOSE PUBLISHING CO., LLC
A Christian Based Book Publishing Platform

Eccl. 3:11 (GW) It is beautiful how God has done everything at the right time.

WRITING WITH A PURPOSE

(205)336-2277
www.divinepurposepublishing.com
info@divinepurposepublishing.com

DiVINE PURPOSE PUBLISHING CO., LLC
A DOBBS FUSION COMPANY

EVERYDAY LOW PRICES
WWW.DIVINEPURPOSEPUBLISHING.COM

	Basic	Deluxe	The Works	Extreme
reg.	$1099	$1999	$3849	$6999
	$899	$1699	$3299	$5599